Spare a Thought

A poetry collection

by Jenny Symons

Spare a Thought

By Jenny Symons

© 2017 Jenny Symons
ISBN: 9781912092697

First published in 2017 by Arkbound Ltd (Publishers).
No part of this publication may be reproduced, stored in a retrieval system, or transmitted, in any form or by any means without the prior permission of the publisher, nor be otherwise circulated in any form of binding or cover other than that in which it is published and without a similar condition being imposed on the subsequent purchaser.

Arkbound is a social enterprise that aims to promote social inclusion, community development and artistic talent. It sponsors publications by disadvantaged authors and covers issues that engage wider social concerns. Arkbound fully embraces sustainability and environmental protection. It endeavours to use material that is renewable, recyclable or sourced from sustainable forest.

Arkbound
Backfields House
Upper York Street
Bristol BS2 8QJ
England

www.arkbound.com

For love, peace and happiness

Foreword by the Publisher

A good publisher should maintain an impartial, professional relationship with their authors. With this book, however, that principle has not been possible to uphold.

Sometimes you encounter people in life who are like stars in a pitch black sky; whose love, kindness and compassion know no bounds - despite the pain they have suffered themselves. Never dealing out judgment, always seeing the good in others, these souls are rare in society's cruel stream. You may never know them, or one could be sitting by you right now. Perhaps, secretly, a bit of their light shines in all of us.

Rarer still is it to find such people basking in awards, honours and acclaim. They are content to be unknown and uncelebrated. That is why this book's foreword has not been written by the author, or by some celebrity, and why its very existence is owed as much to chance as to human endeavour.

Whether it is chance or fate which shapes this life is a question only you can decide. These poems explore such conundrums, whilst showing the author's heart-rending journey through hospitalisation due to schizophrenia, towards freedom and discovery, providing insights for us all.

If ever words could drift above pages, emulating the white in which they are born, may these poems be as a light unto your world.

Spare a Thought

Spare a thought for those who care—
Amid the wars and life's chaos there is time to spare,
Time to think and see and hear,
Time to feel things deeply without fear.

Spare a thought for each flower that grows,
The beauty of the sky, each gust of wind that blows,
Watch the delicate wings of a bird fly by
And listen to the love and beauty in its cry.

Spare a thought for those who starve,
While others stand and watch the meat we carve,
And think of each prisoner alone in his cell,
The steps of society – whose fault is it he fell?

Spare a thought for the lovely and afraid,
Drug addicts, meth drinkers, and all who have strayed,
Think of the warmth and security of the fireside,
While others, homeless, stumble in the cold outside.

Spare a thought for humanity to care—
We are all thoughts with time to spare,
Remember, with hope, the sun always shines,
Although it is hidden by clouds sometimes.

A Human Manifesto

Lately I frequently burst into tears
When nights seem at peace.
For now the wealth of one's soul, one fears
It hasn't a grain to release:
No one needs it.
In search of the idiot
You wear yourself out in a day!
After work people go
After money and whores.
Why not?
I shall make my way alone
In a mass of human ice,
Glittering like a precious stone,
Unique among foes,
Skies!
I want to shine.
Let my soul shelter its gems at night
Along the velvet line of your black dress.
Ministers, leaders, papers – they lie!
Stand up,
Unbend your backs
From prostration.
See – the pellets of atoms of death
Are floating over the graves.
Arise!

Arise!
Arise!
Inflamed rebellious blood!
Forward, destroy and finish it off –
This rotting prison of State!
Tread the corpses of cowards
Bringing black bombs,
Like plums,
For the hungry,
Spread them on trays
of a meeting place.
Where are they?
Those whom we need.
Those who will freeze the trigger,
Those who will cut out the ulcers of war
with mutiny's sacred dagger.
Where are they?
Where are they?
Where are they?
They may not exist.
Over there –
You see their shadows
Welded to lathers
By coins clenched in a fist.
Man disappeared.
Worthless, a fly.
Scarcely moving through lines in a book.
I'll stand in a square

And hammer a scream of despair
Into the city's big ear...
And then I'll press my revolver
Hard on the temple...
No one will tread
The white, shredded veil
Of my soul.
People!
Leave me, forget it...
Don't bother to comfort,
There is nothing to breath with
In your inferno!
Welcome famine and paltriness now!
And I, in the gutter,
Spit at your mighty city of iron
Cramped, full of money and dirt.
Skies!
I can't give account
Of all that I do...
Give me a knife to chastise!
Can you see someone painting
Black lines on the white?
Can you see
How dark at dusk
Grits in its teeth
A bloodstained flag?
And life terrifies like a jail,
Built on human phosphorate.

Falling!
Falling!
Falling!
Grow bold instead of me.
I have no wish to feed on carrion
And so conform;
I have no wish to pick the fruits
Off graves to satisfy my labouring guts.
I don't want your bread:
The dough was mixed with tears.
I fall,
And I soar higher,
Sober in delirium,
Awake in my sleep…
And I feel humanity
Spreading its blossom in me,
We are used to
Looking at faces,
While taking a stroll in the streets
With time all our own,
And see them befouled
By life, like your own.
And then –
Like thunder,
Like the appearance of Christ,
Trampled, crucified, crushed,
Rises the beauty of man.
It is I,

Calling to Justice,
Calling to rise.
No longer wishing to serve,
I tear to pieces the fetters,
You cast in your lies.
It is I,
Shackled by laws,
Proclaiming a human manifesto!
I give my heart to the ravens,
Let them peck out a cross.

Life

What is life? Is it but a dream
which floats across a sky of eternity?
What is the purpose of such a dream,
shrouding us in clouds of illusion?
Why are we floating down a river of time
towards an intangible sea called death?
Some unknown destiny before us,
beyond any reach of imagination.

Who is God? Is he but a dream
created by our mysterious minds,
as part of the unreality within ourselves
to shield loneliness with security?
Perhaps they speak with truth,
who say God lives eternally,
and life flows on within our souls?
My truth is dreams for peace of mind.

Clouds

As I watch the crimson-tinted clouds above,
they float like dreams across the sky;
they glide like pure white fleece,
intangible shapes of changing beauty
blended with wondrous wisps of vapour.

I see tinted hues from purple mountains,
dreamy shades of blue-green seas,
harmonised to fuse with the eternal sky.

The whispering secret of clouds haunts me,
their magical fantasy too:
Are they cushions for the angels?
Or lost souls led by soothing winds
towards the unknown destiny of God?

~ ~ ~

There is a place for me
but where is the key?
The cold iron bars are rusting,
the empty uncertainty awaiting
like a hidden shadow at the door.

~ ~ ~

Hope in the Sun

Freedom is at last awakening,
my heart is lifted, my voice is singing –
a sound of music fills the air,
as the golden sun glistens through my hair.
This music says a thousand things,
releasing unknown feelings as it rings.
Happiness glows like the gleaming sun,
fear is gone – no longer I run.
Here I face the future alone and steadfast,
into the air my troubles are cast,
they are now no more than a wisp in the wind,
for my pathway to freedom leaves them all behind.

~ ~ ~

*Illusions are real and reality an illusion,
our pretences as sincere as our sincerity –
a hard truth.*

~ ~ ~

By a Waterfall

Far away lies the noisy hustle of the distant world,
further still the echoing voices
      of humanity are hurled.
Here I stand, head in hand on a bank
      by the riverside.
The chilled wind blows sluggishly through
      the nettles where I hide.
My heart is full of sadness, grief untold,
amongst the whistling whirl of water,
the tragic turbulent turn of water,
as it glistens and gleams in the sun.

The H Bomb

The sky is darkening,

the clouds are threatening,

no longer is the world alive,

we are now like bees in a hive

struggling to survive.

The bomb has fallen.

Too late, my friends, for love,

for jealousy and hate overrule the dove.

~ ~ ~

Sometimes the sun shines
and dries the tears in my eyes,
but the sun cannot shine for ever.

Sometimes the rain falls
in sympathy with my tears
but the rain cannot fall for ever.

Sometimes the sky is black
and all people are asleep
but I cannot live for ever.

~ ~ ~

Dreams

Dreams unfold a world of beauty,
A life intangibly secure
within a shroud of illusion.
Life is but a dream
which floats like clouds
and glows like fire
across a sky of eternal time.

Why should such dreams exist?
And life be masked by insecurity?
Are we human beings
like germinating seeds,
searching for the sunlight,
nourished with tears of rain
which falls in the shadow of death?

Dreams will live eternally
as the essence of our souls,
alight with misty illumination,
Life's spiritual treasure,
as one with God forever.

I Long For…

I long for freedom – freedom in my mind,
to tear apart the mask of fearful life,
and see a world of wondrous dreams
within the haunting magic of my soul.

I long to wander – wander far away
across the purple-shrouded distant hills,
through lonely mists of silver haze
towards the peaceful skies beyond.

~ ~ ~

Time marches on
the tide turns and retreats
from the gentle sands
like a spirited horse
with mane and tail flown

~ ~ ~

Love

The gentle hues of silver skies

touch my mind and fill my eyes;

my heart is full with joyous urge,

my mind cries forth with gentle surge.

All within me melts like rain

but I myself am fiery flame,

Freedom comes as a flying bird,

my voice cries out for I have heard;

it is the silent song of wondrous love,

which sings like the freedom of a dove.

A Spider Web in the Morning

It stood there in the grass
Shining, radiant, with hundreds of coloured balls;
Yellow, green, blue and red.
Shivering slightly under bending bows of grass
Drying their backs in the sun,
A maze of tiny threads
Dangling in the air;
Masterly, architectural work,
Hanging, blown about,
Soft like a misty shield.

~ ~ ~

Slowly, silently…
retracing the steps…
Sadly remembering
all those before us
… thinking
soon I'll have to
walk forward again…

~ ~ ~

~ ~ ~

I am but a speck of dust
blown about in the wind…
A minute particle
existing in a mass…
… yet alone …
We are all alone … individuals
We? … the specks of life …
Look at the sky…
… the sea …
… the mountains …
then believe me
We are but tiny specks of dust
in a vast universe… unknown…
Far greater and magnificent
than we could ever imagine ourselves to be

~ ~ ~

Living

Slow bleak awakening from the morning dream
Brings me in contact with the sudden day
I am alive – this I.
I let my fingers drift along my body
Realization warns them, and my nerves
Prepare their rapid messages and signals
While memory begins recording codeine
Repeating; all the time imagination
Mutters, you'll only die.

I think of others who awaken,
And wander if they go out to meet the morning
More valiantly than I;
Not asking of this day if they will be living,
What have I done that I should be alive?
Oh, can I not forget that I am living?

Cool pasture, living tree, tall corn, great
Cliff or languid sleeping sand, cold sea, waves,
Rivers running,
Give me content while I can think of you;
Give me your living breath… or back to my drugs -
                                            death.

Money

Just pieces of crumpled paper
Small round coins
Marked with the face of 'Her Majesty'
What majesty?
So small and insignificant
Yet why should it be so important?

What is money?
What is life?
Life is the sun… the wind… the sea
People who feel love and happiness
People who feel sorrow and pain
Money is… ? … nothing
Why must it be so important in our lives?

~ ~ ~

Someday… one day
We'll find a way…
… Follow the sun …
… Everyone run …
… Leave the world alone …
… Live …

The Fountain

A gushing force of water rising, rising
spaying out in the darkness
Minute particles of fresh white light
bubbling… dissolving in the air
Crystal clear – ice cold –
yet warm and friendly.
Colours so beautiful swirling round
Creating patterns, changing continuously
into even more beauty…
The sound of sparkling pure water
from deep within the earth
I gazed with spiritual wonder
I touched… and felt…
Something beautiful happened…
I was now part of this unknown beauty
… my spirit within was shared with
… The Fountain of Life …

A Seed

A tiny seed barely visible to the eye
… a shoot bursts the crust …
and grows up towards the light
… light is life …
A fresh green stem
branching out above the ground
growing – growing towards the light
… light is life …
Small green leaves
unfold their delicate beauty
reaching out to the sky
… light is life …
The stem grows and grows
buds rise and open
petals transparent and fragile
A flower is born
… light is life …

The Sea

Forward – retreating
Creating – destroying
an endless sorrowful sound
yet full of the joy of its existence.
Rising out of a grey waving mass
Rising nearer it curves
a mass of bubbly froth
Speeding nearer, nearer
to pause gently and gather up its strength
then fall back to rise again
… Forward – retreating …
… Creating – destroying …

If Only

If only you knew what's inside of me
there would be no need for hate…
no need for your questions and frowns…
If only you knew what's inside of me now
then you too would understand…
let your feelings flow away
dissolve all that hate with love…
love of life, love of love
peace will surely be yours
If only you knew what's inside of me.
…If only I knew what's inside of you now.

~ ~ ~

A flower's beauty grows
Share that beauty and there is love
love of life
love surrounds you
dissolve all that hate in the world
with the love within you
then peace will surely be yours
from the love of a flower.

~ ~ ~

Suicide?

Who are you?

I am me.

Who is me?

The person I am.

How do you know you are a person?

I only know I am me.

What are you?

A feeling.

Then why do you have a body?

It's something given to enable me to discover experiences.

What experiences?

The experiences we have to go through to find ourselves.

When do you know yourself?

When you have peace of mind.

So when you have peace of mind you don't need your body anymore?

No …

Drop Out?

Out where?
In a land of dreams
which are apart from your world
Your world exists like mine
Your reality is strong and hard
My reality is weak
I cannot be so real
because reality frightens me
Please don't condemn me
for what I am …

~ ~ ~

Eyes watching, waiting
in the corners of my mind
Piercing, striking…
then retreating steadily
when they find nothing is there

~ ~ ~

Despair

Empty spaces
clouds of illusion
visions of love and hate
long since gone from my mind
… there is nothing left …
Where has it all gone?
Those hours of joy and bitter anger
no longer haunt me
only ghosts and spirits are there
controlling what I do and say.
Go life – go go go.

~ ~ ~

I am?
I am what I am – they say.
How do they know?
They are not me.

~ ~ ~

Prison

Sitting here alone in my cold cell
Gazing at the barred window
and huge iron door
slammed, locked with jingling keys
I wonder what it's like to be free again
To see the sun
feel its warm rays
and wander free in the fields and shore
… to hear the song of birds …
Loneliness haunts me
tugging at my heart in despair
Sitting here in my prison cell
I wonder how much my freedom is worth.

~ ~ ~

Fly away little bird
your nest is no longer here
the wind has blown the warm feathers
and twigs away
and only the branches remain
but you have strong wings
so fly little bird – fly.

~ ~ ~

Time Wheel

The wheels of time steadily turn—
the huge waterwheel of the universe—
a never-ending flow of life winds on
to the hum of seconds, hours, days, years,
each one creating and destroying,
each turn the vital move to life
for yesterday has already gone
and taken its happiness and despair;
yet the waterwheel flows on.

~ ~ ~

Sometimes I wonder what freedom really is,
for every day has its own restrictions;
'work away today – live your life tomorrow',
so they say and tomorrow never comes,
and who are they to know,
they are never free;
what is freedom to them and me?
Their freedom may be different – it is.
They? – society – never free
from the restrictions of their words.
Me? my freedom is oblivion.

~ ~ ~

The Nurse

Further and further into the depths of despair,
darkness fills her sad heart.
Every day I open her door with a smile,
trying to bring joy into her grief;
beneath her crippled body
I reflect the strength and determination,
tears that flow in her efforts.
Despite her pain I see a smile,
life flows on inside her heart,
in streams of warm remembrance of her youth.
Oh that I might lift that crust of pain
and let her have her freedom again.

~ ~ ~

Shining globules of misty haze
Silver threads of transparent glaze
She rises out of splendour
through soft rays of moonlight
Shivering slightly in the coolness of the night.
Across the sea a lonely seagull cries
waves ripple gently where she flies
Gliding slowly in the beauty of the night
her shadow slides out of sight.

In Bed

Wisps of dreamy haze
life and long forgotten daze
Brightly reaming hours pass away
Here safe in bed I lay
Life passes gently by me
a cloud in the mind's eye
today and tomorrow loom ahead
but life is unreal and happy in bed.

~ ~ ~

Why do I smile
when underneath I'm miserable?
Why do I laugh
when deep down I'm crying?
Why do people say things to me
which make me curl up inside?
Why does everything seem so futile
when I awake each morning?

~ ~ ~

Will

Wound up like a time bomb
waiting to explode
turning over and over inside
I try to pause and think
confusion fills my mind
they are all out there waiting to pounce
I am too weak to fight much longer
I can only give in to their feelings
but mine are far stronger.
I know inside is my volcano
bubbling, boiling, waiting to erupt
out of all the fantasies one thing remains:
a strength, a will power
even though it is confused
something inside too strong to hold
yet fear grips hold of me
when I know where it will all end.

~ ~ ~

I don't know what is real
I can't touch what I feel
I wander around without direction
I have to search til I find myself.

~ ~ ~

Hold My Hand

All I wish for is you to hold my hand

to listen to me and try to understand

I am lost in the depths of the sea

my legs are weary and I've blown my mind on drugs.

I want someone to hold my hand

and try to understand.

But it is a wild world

and few people stop to think

because they are too busy with their own lives.

Reflections, Illusions

I don't want to work away
doing just what they all say –
'Work hard girl, and you will find
Someday you'll have a job like mine.'
Every day they show me up,
frighten me with their domineering,
as though I am no one
and they can overrule me
telling me what to do and say.
Why don't they let me be for a change?
All I ask is to be let alone in life
and not to be dominated by them
and everything I do, watched and criticised.
I am a person in my own right,
I have my failings and misgivings
just like everyone else,
but I am not here to be taken over by them,
whoever they are.

~ ~ ~

My life stretches out like a railway line
but the locomotive is in my head.

~ ~ ~

We Must Try

Searching beyond despair
to find peace and tranquillity somewhere,
I look beyond people's faces
to mountains and far away places.
Why is there so much hate in the world?
Why do people destroy all their love
and burden each other with hate?
Life is hard to understand
but we must try to go through it hand in hand.

Voices

Voices piercing through me
fill my mind with fear,
they threaten to overpower me
and force me to do things against my will.
Where do they come from?
I can only see that their invisible bodies
are evil and threatening to me.
They wish to overrule myself,
control everything I do and say.
So I must shrink away from them
and build up strength inside me,
So I have the willpower
to turn the voices away.

Searching

Searching through despair
beyond all my tears
towards an unknown destiny before me,
my life passes by the face of time.
Shadows of night
Drift by into day
and dreams of the day
dance and leap in confusion.
I don't know what is real,
I can't touch what I feel,
and I hide behind the shield of my illusion.

~ ~ ~

Like a snail in its shell
my home is always above me
I retreat inside
when fear surrounds me.
Alone in darkness
Knowing the fear outside
my shell protects me.

~ ~ ~

A Spring Day

Here I sit listening to the birds
as they sing through the clear spring air.
A butterfly lands, like a song,
on the bright vivid yellow of a gorse blossom
which bursts like happiness from the grass.
The fields, like soft patchwork, surround me
and a fresh gentle breeze caresses me.
The freedom of nature touches my heart;
here alone I pull myself apart,
like the purple-tinted wisps of cloud above.
As I watch the wings of a bird pass by,
I wonder deep inside at the beauty of her cry.
No noise of echoing, tortuous traffic
and forcefulness of people breaking up the day;
here alone I face myself
amid the peaceful beauty of a Spring Day.

The Sun

Warm bright rays from overhead
She shines in all her splendour
Like a ball of fire
A furnace from above
My god is the sun
I worship her and long for her beauty and power
Everything within me dissolves with her splendour.

~ ~ ~

As my feet drift across the stretch of sand,
the gentle wind caresses the sun across my face,
I watch every wave, a froth of sparkling white,
turn and break, speeding steadily for the shore.
Life is like a wave continuously swirling,
beautiful in its bubbly colours
and breaking with vivid pressure
only to pause and suddenly turn back
toward the ocean, so mysteriously full of power.

~ ~ ~

Tuke Ward, Digby Hospital

Pacing up and down... up and down...
Forward and back... forward and back...
Keys jingle... doors are locked.
Trees sway in the breeze outside,
I watch behind a sheet of glass.
Sunlight warms through,
yet to me a deadly glow.
LARGACTIL time.
I move my weary body,
my mind staggers again,
then my robot legs walk me to a bed,
restless turmoil with the heat of the night—
my eyes close... a safe corner... alone.

Fighting Back Tears

Sometimes I wonder how my life goes on;
Day by day I sit in darkness
Afraid to move beyond that shroud of despair.
There is a place for me but where is the key?
A door of bitterness confronts me,
Words bite past my ears,
Stinging slightly, I hold the tears back.
My love, like a strength within me fights and wins yet
another battle for hope that conflicts inside me,
And yet again the love wins
But next time – will there be another one?
Those tears might not hold back.

~ ~ ~

How can I go forward when
I don't know which way I'm facing?
Why must every step bring despair?
Each day brings its unhappiness
mounting up inside steadily
until I can no longer hold it, but burst
and freak out into the atmosphere
until everything inside is exhausted.

~ ~ ~

Autumn

Leaves crisp and golden
fall gently in the cold breeze
so light and fragile they fly with ease
to land here at my feet, yet far away
their life forgotten but mine to stay.

As time passes their shapes mould with age,
each delicate skeleton will soon be gone.
But I can see that beauty now,
I don't know why, I don't know how.

~ ~ ~

The haunting cry of a lonely seagull
soaring higher; it flies above the jagged cliffs,
I watch the sparkling foam of the sea,
bubbles of glistening water, fresh and pure.
Laying back in the sand, I close my eyes
and listen to the peaceful swirl of each wave,
a never-ending symphony of nature.

~ ~ ~

Life and Man

How long can man live on
amidst all this pain and sin?
Can't he see the folly of his ways,
must he desecrate the beauty of this world?

What has happened to the songs of the birds?
The very warmth and joy of Spring?
Must every innocent, fragile flower disappear
beneath the rubble of our lives?

Can no man hear the fury of the waves
with their message of power and awe?
No man can understand nature's wrath
whatever he might do.

Is it because we are afraid
to admit our own inadequacy?
That we cannot acknowledge higher things
therefore we must destroy them,
every one?

Peace and Rest

Under this tree, where light and shade
Speckle the grass like a thrushes breast,
Here, in the grass, this green and quiet place,
I'll give myself to peace and rest.

The peace of my contented mind
That is to me a wealth untold –
When the moon has no more silver left
And the sun is at the end of his gold.

Butterflies

As butterflies are but winged flowers
half sorry for their change,
so still and long they lie on leaves,
they would be thought flowers again –
Even so my thoughts, that should expand
and grow to higher themes above,
return like butterflies to lie
on the old things I love.

Rain

The dark grey thunderclouds roll across the sky
to herald some strife in heaven
which makes the sky so troubled.
As the raindrops begin to fall,
each pearl so clear and fresh,
they seem to stream like tears from the sky.

Oh rain, what beauty to behold!
For life revolves around your glittering crystals,
Gentle gems of water dissolve in tiny cells
and life flows on within us and about us.
Who sent this wondrous gift of life?
We as raindrops will return to Him
and rain will fall eternally.

Mother Earth

Have you ever touched the colours of a rainbow
or really listened to the song of a bird?
Have you ever stopped to let a snail
cross your path unharmed?
Or really listened to the sound of silence?
Why must our lives be ruled
by the roar of cars and TV,
buses, planes, record players
blasting propaganda to our minds.
Mother Earth calls to us unheard –
we pollute our rivers, oceans and streams,
we cut down trees in the rainforests,
we pollute our atmosphere,
we make more and more insecticides
and bleaches for our toilets and floors
to take away the guilt by having
'nice clean homes' –
meanwhile Mother Earth's cry calls to us unheard.
Why must our children suffer all this,
with computerised toys
instead of sticks and earth and water?
Meanwhile Mother Earth's cry calls to us unheard.
She will go on calling
till she has no strength –
when the last drop of bleach

has killed the last living organism in our rivers,
when the fumes from our car exhausts
have polluted the air,
when there are no more trees left to cut down,
we will still have our 'clean disinfected boxes' to live in
but there will be nothing else and we will die
because Mother Earth's cry called to us unheard.
We were too busy listening to the politicians
arguing who should be in power
and greedily finding ways of making more money—
meanwhile Mother Earth called to us unheard.